The
Ninth Pawn

A BOOK OF UNWRITTEN VERSES

# of White

The Ninth Pawn

A BOOK OF UNWRITTEN VERSES

of White

VIJAY FAFAT

WALKING STICK PUBLICATION

WALKING STICK PUBLICATION

ISBN-13: 978-981-11-5677-9

Published by Walking Stick Publication, Singapore

Book concept - Vijay Fafat
Image selection - Vijay Fafat
Book layout - Chandan Crasta

First Printing: October, 2017

"We are all names
penciled in a forgotten book . . .
. . . waiting. . .
waiting to jump out of the pages . . . "

FOREWORD

The inimitable Borges had his internal anguish writ large in *Matthew XXV: 30* :

> *"In vain have oceans been squandered on you,*
> *in vain the sun, wonderfully seen through Whitman's eyes.*
> *You have used up the years and they have used up you,*
> *and still, and still, you have not written the poem."* [1]

We all hear this inner urging at some stage in life. Away from our vocational responsibilities, removed from the quotidian worries and preoccupation, we all strive to write our literal or metaphorical poems, in our own ways, following our own passions. The search for meaning keeps enticing us even when the plebeian life supplies us with all which we outwardly seek. In this, we are the musk deer which cannot fathom the secret of the heavenly fragrance perpetually shrouding it, and hunts for its source ceaselessly in all six directions, not knowing that the unwrapping of the riddle lies close to its heart, within its belly; a secret which shadows it literally and lets it not rest in peace.

To unravel our cryptogram, we must pick up the thread somewhere, since:

> *The End tugs at The Beginning:*
> "Start! For I must find my expression!"

Almost afraid of having Borges' Infinite Voice catching up with its finger-wagging admonishment, and in an effort to hold it at bay, here then is my first effort at gathering up the oceans which have been squandered on me by a generous world...

Chess is a game of few rules but infinite flight of fancy. Mathematically precise, but given to unpredictably rich patterns of evolution, it has an air of unwinding mystery and apocalyptic secrets. One can find expressions of daily life as well as metaphorical representations of human foibles in the decisions and movements of its rooks, its queens, its bishops, its pawns. Their diagonal movements, mischievous sparring, lurking attacks, inscrutable plans and intransigent blockades are representations of our

[1]From "Jorge Luis Borges - Selected Poems", edited by Alexander Coleman

recurring histories and complex futures. They are models of our cunning and naïveté, our planned vision and myopic blind spots, all in one microcosmic arcade of 64 squares.

Not satisfied with the cornucopia offered by the 8-by-8 planar board of black and white, restless minds have explored chess in 3-D, on spherical and toroidal surfaces, on hexagonal and circular boards, in multi-player settings, rapid-fire formats, blind-folded demonstrations, and with such fancy variations as "*Alice Boards*" and "*Atomic Chess*".

The ninth pawn of white (or black, for that matter) is a figurative variation on this theme. It is not allowed in the rules of standard chess. It remains non-existent; a fantasy; a breaking of the rules in its appearance. Perhaps it is a desire of the "white" side - "*oh! for the want of one more pawn!*". Or it may be an iota of disagreement we inflate into a long-exhausted argument. The ninth pawn is versatile in its hovering potentiality.

The ninth pawn is also philosophical, living only at the corner of the eye as a minor startling occurrence when first conjured. It is of no consequence in the evolution of the actual game, but as other minor desires of life, it remains a snagging in the back of our minds. There are times we wish the ninth pawn existed "on our side"; there are times it seems the "other side" has unfairly inherited an army of ninth pawns. It is a matter of narrow perspectives.

The verses in this collection are similar. They are simple drops of incipient thought; incomplete emotions looking for their outlets. By themselves, they are of limited consequence, like the ninth pawn, and left to their devices, they might well merge back, un-composed, in the infinite book of unwritten verses. Their flight cannot materialize without the reader's indulgence, and her own interpretations in metaphor of the inspired thought. They are meant to trigger introspection, images, stories, and analytic extensions of what may or may not have been implied, and if they fail in that process - *which many surely will* - it is the failure of the craft, not the art nor the reader.

Some verses are straight shots, delivering final conclusions, but most of them are open to a variety of conclusions in a participative mood. E.g.

> *"Must you open the box of Pandora*
> *just to prove you have found the key?"*

is not just the sorrow of the genie let out of the atom, but a question of everyday life: must we always serve up information in the service of probity or truth if the impact is more deleterious than the accrued gain? As another verse says, *"Sometimes it is better never than late..."*

I have outlined my sole excuse to inflict the collection on you, though the infernal Borgesian voice does not shy from its opposite reprimand:

> *Must we be slaves to this...*
> *...this moment of vanity imposed by others?...*

This book will be consigned to future dust, but perhaps it can leave a verse or two to alight in your memory at a random moment on a quiet afternoon as the magical appearance of your own ninth pawn of white...

Vijay Fafat
Singapore
10 October 2017

Led

He and his fate walk together,
Master and Slave.
In which order,
only time and action tell.

Residue

As the tide of life recedes,
and the crest of foam scatters to the wind,
all that's left on the sand
are dying bubbles of dreams and wishes.

With Cold Water

She douses the flames of desire in my eyes,
and asks why I leave the soiree so thirsty.

It Giveth Only

Do not dispute your thirst of water...
...not with the flowing brook.

Interrogative

Asks, he does…

But Oh!

A question so small…

In lieu of . . .

One cannot become a pundit by proxy.

Quenchless

No completeness in the world,
but endless desires...

Take Hold

Let not fate tarry on you.
Seize it before it carries you.

Chart!

Never mourn the loss of a map.
There remains a world to discover.

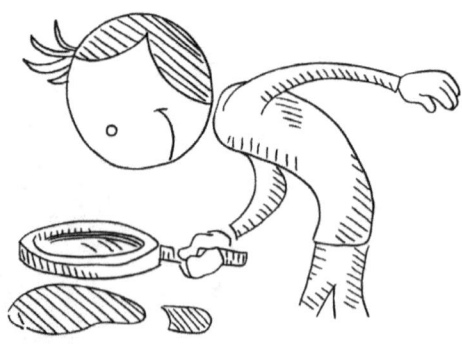

Necessary Vices

Life needs
an essential bargain
of what were once
sacrosanct principles...

Residual

We do not mourn the memories lost.
We mourn the ones which beset us as loyal
friends.

Fast Bait

Trust not the promises of haste.
They curl up as little lies...

Check-mate

The pain of seven continents
weighs on his carefree soul
as God ponders his next move.

Overlooked

Something was said then, I recall,
to move the still spirit.

If only!
Oh, if only I'd heard!
The broken silence
amidst the meaningless mumblings
of my mind.

Through a lens, darkly

Right beneath this shimmering...
beneath this glittering surface of water
lies
a distorted view of the world above.

Senseless . . .

A charlatan walked as a prophet,
and changed the world of sheep in his wake,
and all that while,
God watched
with blind eyes,
helpless…

Advice

The best defense against sarcasm
is to take it literally.

Pusillanimity

Such small doors in such tall houses!
Do Men live here or Pygmies?

Receiver

Speech discriminates between listening ears
even if sound does not.

Where there's one . .

We are slaves
to the dictates of free will.

Left Behind

The past does not forget.
Men do.

Curse

Dawn to dusk, lust to dust,
such is our lot;
we strive for completeness
of the Irrelevant Thought.

The Bugle's Lesson of War and Peace

Listen carefully
to that resonant sound from history;
the embittered, shuffling march
of the troops of Pyrrhus.

Parochial

Ahh, such loss!
Such mortal desires
in the face of immortal offerings!

Sketch it

Draw a gentle sea.
Draw an easy boat.
And row out yonder alone,
against the rising dawn,
to unknown bliss.

Esteem

Thank the imperfections around you,
elevating you in your own eyes.

Nameless

Like a whisper it pervades;
like a perfume it swirls;
even when 'tis just
a memory arrived unbidden...

Pose

A hand raised to strike cannot bless.

Clarity

Meandering words
lose their meaning along the way.

Evolve

From ashes to rose...
...Metamorphose...

Opponent

No cobweb ever stopped
a determined bull.
So it is with doubts,
and thus it is with the seeker...
The choice is simple:
let the other be
beast
or web...

Open Sky

Take flight while you still can, little one.
Let not the sure-footed torrent of naysaying
dampen your wings...

Control

Only a drunkard has a tongue
which moves of its own accord.

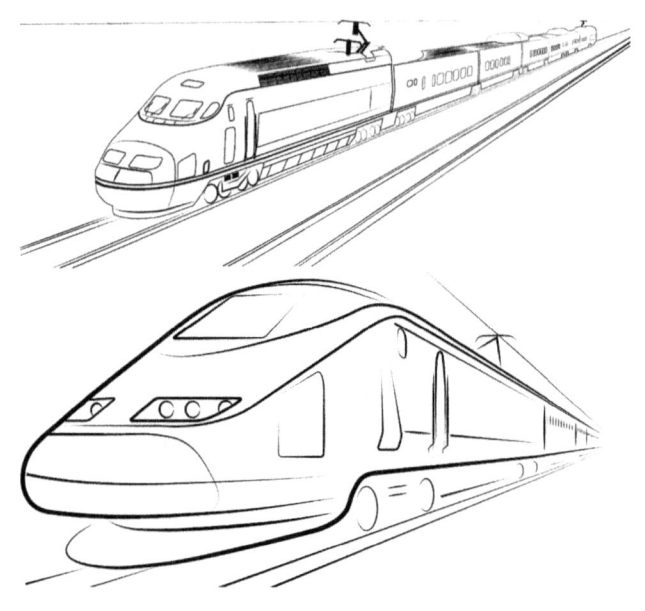

Conference

Must we depart
on these trains of thought
which did not find the station
of uncommon agreement?

Attraction

Locked in combat,
my stare with yours,
seeking that sign…

Tell me, Eyes,
if I'm worthy of your glance,
or your disinterested shrug…

Thoughtlets

Look, a block of words!
Or perhaps,
for the discerning imagination,
a drop of thought...

Unwanted

Sorrow's the name of the heartless Spring
which leaves the cold winter inside...

Card-Game

Are we not a game of Bluff played by life,
till we call, in our death, for a show of hands?

Miasma

Ask not why the air is foul here;
herein dwells the greed of the material world.

False

What manner of pride, that…

…that which raises the head with supplicating eyes…?

Secrets

The memory of first love,
alive in that hidden recess
I visit every morn…
of wistful thoughts,
and rueful regrets…

Beware its Ferality

The baying wolves of vengeance
strain against their leashes,
testing the patience
of civil retribution.

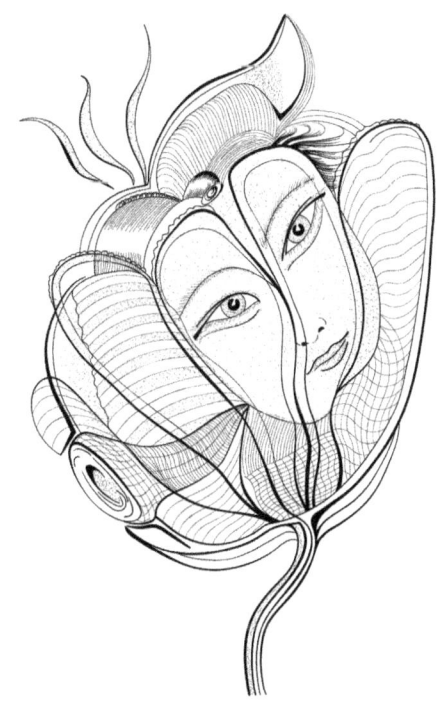

Sartorial Thought

Your conscience is the rough cloth
which covers the nudity of your mind.

Unknowing

The sprinkling of fragrant petals
hid the bed of thorns.
Therein lay their innocent sin...

To make it worse

When heroes make their last stand,
the gods watch.
At times,
the cruelest of them takes an interest…

Inflate

Is it not the case in our daily lives?
We pretend to see a hurricane
in a swirling mote's eye...

Who asks?

The universe
is God's long-hand answer
to a hypothetical question...

Revision

The ink of victory
rewrites history.

Ask Yourself

Is it for name you strive
like an illegitimate off-spring?

Care-free

The blade of grass is insouciant
till it sees an approaching goat.

Work

Stop peeling the skin
from grains of rice.
Do something worthwhile.

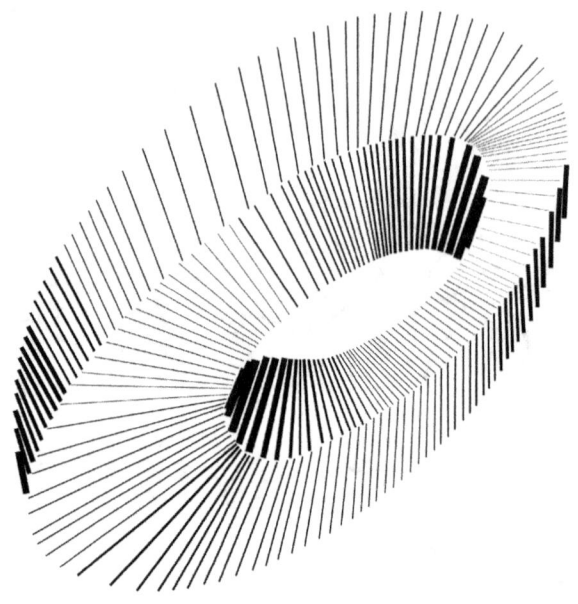

Economy

The brevity of oxymoronic thought...
Such profligacy of parsimony!

Brilliance

Lightning does not explain
nor announce its presence;
the rest of nature must simply take notice.

S. Ramanujan (1887-1920)

$$3 = \sqrt{1 + 2\sqrt{1 + 3\sqrt{1 + 4\sqrt{1 + \cdots}}}}$$

Proof: Define $f(x) = x + n + a$, so that $f(x)^2 = ax + (n + a)^2 + xf(x + n)$.
Set $a = 0$, $n = 1$, $x = 2$ and substitute recursively for $f(x)$.

Give and Take

In any compromise,
the yield of the efforts accrue
only with an equal effort to yield.

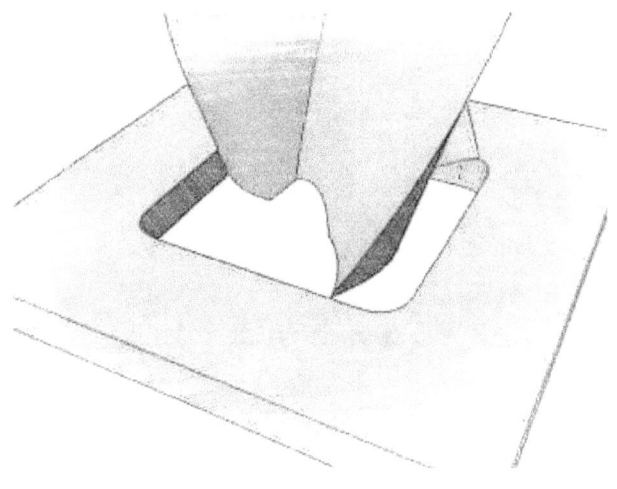

Thinkillate!

If you see a square hole,
don't think of fitting a round peg in it;
ask how the square hole was drilled.

First Hand

He appreciates the true worth of loyalty
who has seen betrayal in person...

Indulge

Grieve not the moment of excess
in a lifetime of moderation.

Alas !

Gone are the days
when stories of magical mythologies
made you feel safe with their promises.

Face Up!

Fate does not wait
on a man's wisdom to deal with it.
It is a bull to be taken by the horns,
lest it tramples you to preordained dust.

Epsilon

Do not frown at an approximation.
You need its friendship everyday.

Armory

Choose your arms with prudence.
Weapons, without caution,
turn on you without loyalty...

Precarious

A man's character is always poised on a slope;
a small nudge,
and gravity takes over.

Viewpoint

A boat: Just a floating piece of wood.
A boat: Art and Ingenuity!

Publish !

Every pen has a story to tell;
if only the eyes of the world listened...

Play it well

We have been written into history already.
All that remains is the unfolding of our acts.

Foundation

On easy sands
do principles shift.

Enigma

Cheap are the words of the mystic;
or profound, maybe…

Arguments

Of what avail,
this flaying of an old ass?
All you ever get
is its petulant braying
and a broken stick.

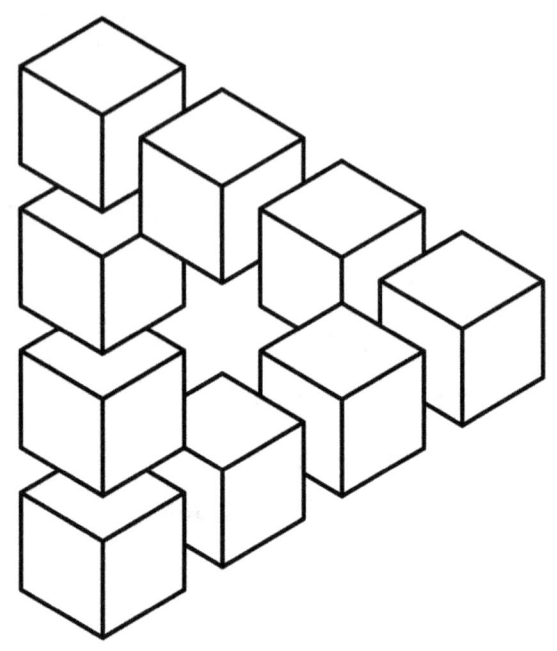

True

An inherent obfuscation
afflicts all difficult truths...

There be Dragons

Mind the abyss between man and humanity;
there sits the dark psyche of the untamed mind...

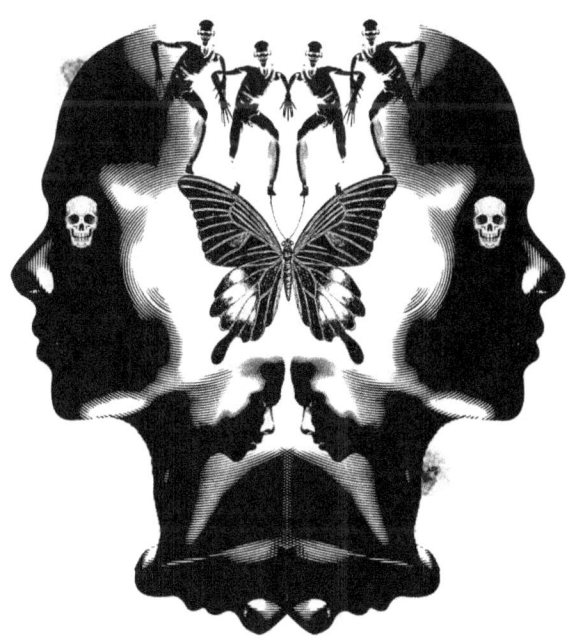

Out of the Ordinary

Anyone can be enchanted by the magical.
True magic belongs
to those mesmerized by the mundane.

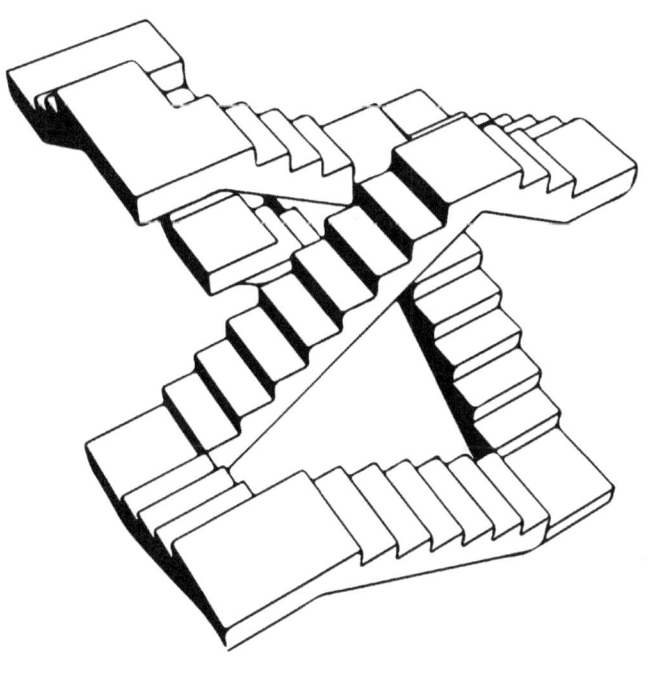

Directional

The staircase of virtue leads
both up and down...

Accept

There is no accounting of the iniquities in life.
There be only grief in maintaining
their perpetual ledger.

Defy

The pen which rebels
signs its symbols for the ages...

1

Rise above the existence
of a simple pronoun...

i

Basic Algebra

Is bad arithmetic,
counting on good intentions alone.

$$1 + 2 = 0$$

Lux

Was it a lamp twinkling in the black of the forest,
or a dot of conscience on a dark heart?

Wavering

A ship out of port
must sail without doubt,
or meet its maker
in the embrace of deep waters.

Vision

It is a small mind which would think
of filling a cup
from the tides of a flood...

Ostrich

It is in our nature
to fortify our errors
against informed correction...

Chaff

What has one gathered
if all one has to show in life
is a collection of regrets?

Denouement

We all hold the Book of Climax.
For most, Destiny turns its pages.
For some - if they choose -
the last pages are redacted,
with the freedom to write at will...

Incommensurate

People can be uncouth incendiary brutes.
To find the needle in the haystack,
they resort to a match-stick.

At First Sight

"Grow old with me!"
his wistful hope spoke out of turn,
resting on a small token
of but a hint of her smile...

Spectators

A thousand eyes watched impassively
the murder of the innocent man
with soulless blindness...

Boorish

A man
of letters few
but words many.

To each unto itself

A wastebasket does not expect
deposits of silver coins.

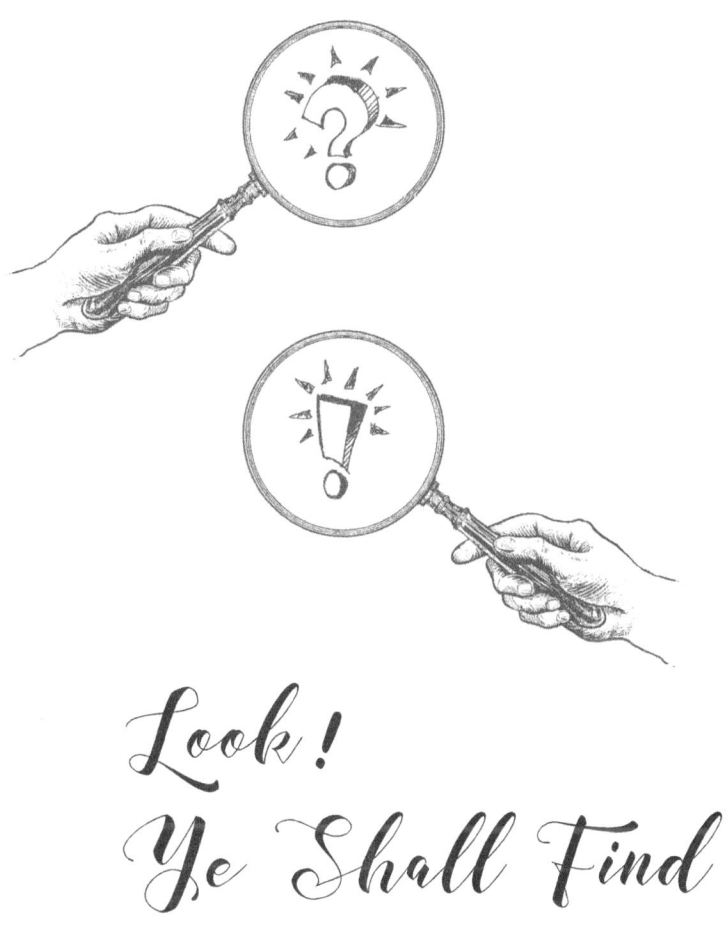

Look!
Ye Shall Find

Often, if one looks, one finds
an interrogative fallen on the path.
Examine it. It may be
a missive from the conscience.

Pun-dit

By his literary sword he rises,
the hero with cutting thoughts...

Ask Yourself

Do we seek truth
or gratification?
Doesn't falsehood,
with its ease of creation,
suffice?

Restraints

With sorrow I break my friendship with you,
Gravity,
for I must reach the stars tomorrow.

A law of Nature

Industry is not the nature of Law.
Slowly they turn,
those wheels of justice...

Modern Man

Where from cometh the rattling?
Ahh, I see him, post-renaissance…
A tin man
with a tin can
storing tin thoughts...

Braggadocio

Don not
a glittering armor
of fatigued metal.

Style

Celebrate moments of great triumph
against a backdrop of quiet humility.

Essential

Every rung contains the soul of the ladder,
and when the last rung is dismantled,
all you are left with
are two wooden beams....
...divorced...

Barn Door

Vigilance!
The bird must shut its beak
once the insect steps inside.

Distillation

The essence of man:
Some deeds,
some thoughts,
a thimbleful of dust...

Egalitarian

"One cannot pretend aristocracy",
they say.
Neither can one feign
the ruggedness of a commoner.

Limit

Logic is brought to its knees
in front of a dull mind,
or undying faith...

The Master

In only mild exaggeration
my mind thinks:
'Borges wrote flowing prose
while the world was learning the alphabet.'

Command

Seek the voice inside,
which only says,
"Seek!"

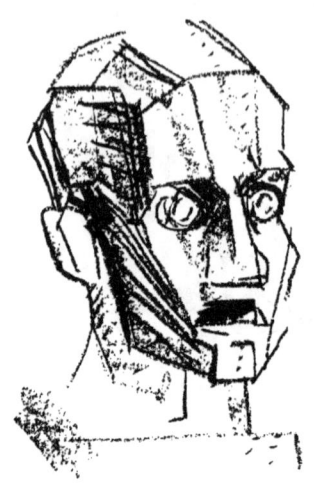

Vanquished

I stand defeated, not knowing it,
in the face of Fate;

For while I revel in my Free Will,
the Future brooks no control...

Easy Habit

Drape your skin with simplicity,
and live comfortably inside it.

Why?

I want to die
Nonymous...

But of course!

It all depends on whose ox did the goring...

Reflected Glory

A pygmy
standing on tall shoulders
remains a pygmy.

Negative Energy

It was the do-nothing pothole which tripped and fell.

It was the guiding road which was hurt.

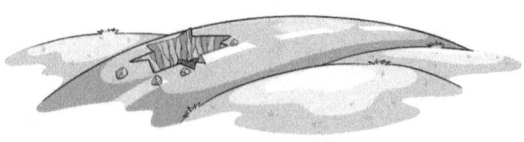

Bequeath

A man rises above the ordinary
when he starts thinking about his legacy.

Moderate

At times,
the spoken word overstates its case.

To My Child

Hold my hand,
and with faith,
Fly...

Child-like

"To the delight of men moves the moon",
suggests the poet.
Oh, such a charming observation!

Cherished

Long in the memory reside
the trivial details of childhood.

Still you do . . .

Why should one feel deceived
when a friend speaks an unkindly truth?

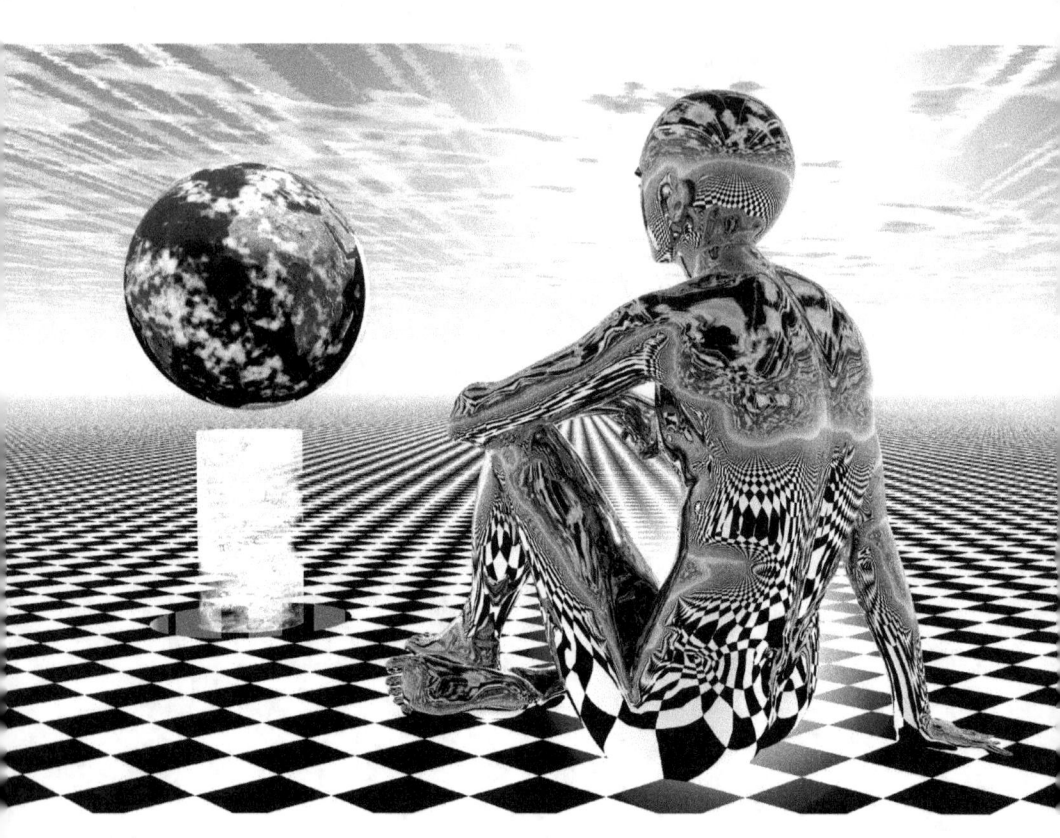

Varnashram

One wonders if the impossible
is merely a limit placed on man
to separate him from the exalted spirits.

Extant

A comforting thought:
that all which remains to be discovered
already exists...

Alas !

A child has passed the threshold of innocence.
There!
There stands a worldly man...

Swept Away

Ahoy there!
Raise the anchor!
Uncheck the drift of the heart,
for here she arrives,
as the torrid flood…

Having lived and not seen

When the last light had brushed his weary eyes,
the last breeze found his final breath;
that was the moment his memory sparked large...
He saw his heaven from his past.

Grasp

I spread my hand
and caught the moon in a pinch.
Such small immensity
from the right perch...

Impulsate !

Let the present moment
take hold of your passions;
there is time enough for the future.

Intentions

The little trivialities of life gather up in weight...
burying all good intentions.

Renewal

Shed not a tear
for the fallen leaves;
'tis the Autumn which heralds
the Spring on the horizon.

Treasures

What regret
for that which slips the fingers?
Wondrous the finds
held back in the grasp…

Borrowed

In all its beaming pride the moon rose,
blissfully unaware,
shining in reflected glory.

Scripture Rapture

In solitude open your mind like a book;
there is wonder between those covers.

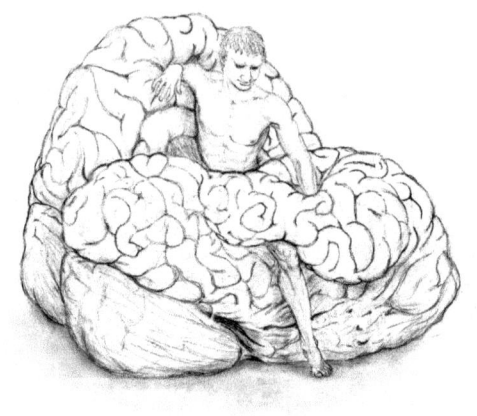

Wondrous

It is not everyday
that one dreams of Reality.
Seize that thought
when the moment befalls.

Palette

One always colors the truth;
never it stays black or white.

What shade of truth, that?

A Dare

Roll aside the carpet
under which you've hidden
the inconvenient truths...

Method Actor

He who cries,
suffering understands.

Identity

Be the corners
which bend lines to their will.

I AM
STRONGER
than Fear.

— Malala
Yousafzai

Make-believe

Gods and Demons.
Mere beings of imagination,
subject to the whims and caprice
of collective will,
of social dreams,
of mortal fears
of superstition...

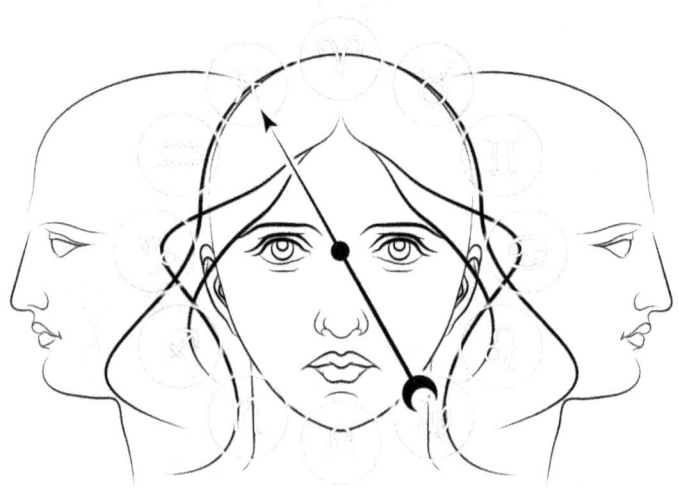

Allure

The mystery of a book endures
while its covers are unread.

Partial Amnesia

The memory is a mirror,
stealing its reflections selectively.

Bleat

Rail against the style shepherds.
Don't be too much of a conforming goat.

Appearances

Let us pretend that all is as was deigned,
for to behave otherwise would be ugly.

Kaliyug

No one lives
by truth on his tongue,
or fealty on his mind.
These are the signs
of our inherited times...

Fear?

A bull with two horns
appears an opportunity to a matador.

Couch Potato

A potted plant might appreciate it
if the pot got up and walked around
once in a while.

Sadly . . .

We need no ghosts or ghouls.
There are men of dark talents.

Dearly Departed

Once upon a time,
Common Sense was a commoner's leader.
On a dark day,
the mobs assassinated him.

Obligation

Is the failure of conviction
necessarily the fault of the believer?
Does not the canon owe
a responsibility of veracity to its followers?

The Slow Orchard

Salvation does not appear at request or demand.
The fruits of penance ripen at their pace.

Imagine in a Dream

Stand still at a pointed precipice,
a prisoner to your balance,
and smile at the abyss,
before it claims your long fall...

KURT GÖDEL (1906–78)

AUSTRIAN-BORN US philosopher and mathematician Kurt Gödel is most famous for his incompleteness theorems (1931), which revolutionized logic. Gödel showed that in any formal system (a symbolic system based on axioms), there exist propositions that are undecidable (they can neither be proved nor disproved). Most importantly, the consistency of the axioms themselves cannot be proved. Gödel's work has had a profound impact on how mathematicians think about their subject. In particular, it shows why the attempts of David Hilbert, Bertrand Russell, and others to create a purely axiomatic foundation for mathematics must fail.

Epiphany

Oh! To die
without understanding
Godel's theorem!
For want of another life,
for need of another mind...

Self-aware under a Bodhi Tree

We are all scrambled pieces of a puzzle,
and have limited time to put them together.
To die having completed the picture,
that is the way of Buddha.

Downhill

The agony of fulfillment...
for all paths lead away in time...

For the Pilgrim

The traveler's tunnel passeth through earth,
Hades and Heaven alike...

Imagine That!

Humans…

Alive.
Sentient.
Fabulously unpredictable.

We are the stuff of fables
for the Other Realm…

Obviously

When the horse is unwilling,
there's little the hay-wagon can do.

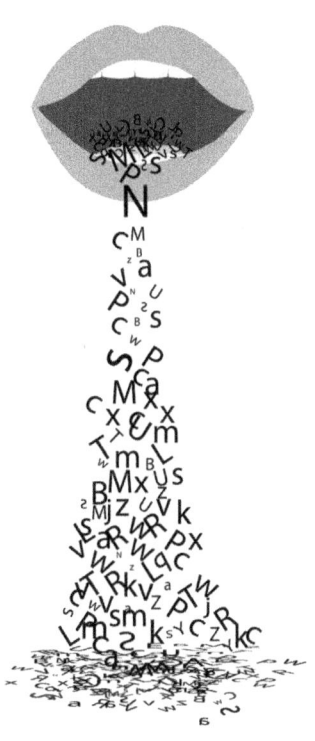

Unscattered

Of what import your pronouncements,
when words fall at your feet,
not to be borne by the winds,
to the four corners of land's end?

What else?

An anticipation there is in life...
For you...

Cost

A rising balloon expanding with pride;
sooner than later pays its price...

Set Aside . . .

Let us not discourage ourselves.
Let not the minor pebbles of doubt
dissuade the endeavors to move the mountains.

Eruditorium

In these frothing waters of grey bubbles,
hot air passes for erudition...

Religion

Is she a God
if She is someone else's god?

Semantics

Is it envy I feel,
or disappointment in myself?

Healer

Where be the loom,
to weave a blanket of peace,
on the shivering, bruised body of war?

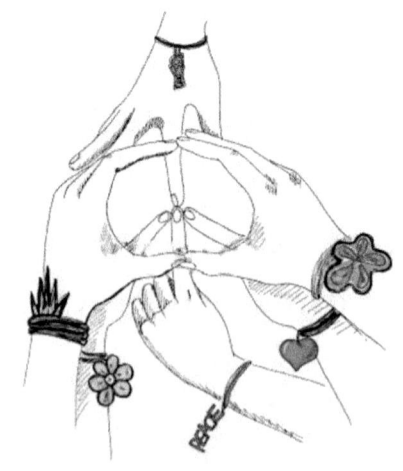

Source-coded

A reflection may promise fidelity,
but never perfection.

Row !

Idle oars tread no waves;
lazy hands maroon the skiff.

So One Thinks

With a sigh of relief
pent up for a millennium,
the sage tree fell straight,
but not a sound it made,
in the absence of someone to hear it.

Unilateral

A mirror shows but one side.

In the Beginning . . .

An epic.
A fable.
A single word.

Immolation

A moth casts away its self-esteem
in a meaningless act of masochism,
facing the unrequiting love
of a Circean flame.

Tea Leaves

In the patterns of time
is written the fate of history...

Go-Getter

One does not wait upon an adventure;
none ever arrives.
You must meet it on its own turf,
or make peace with a phlegmatic life.

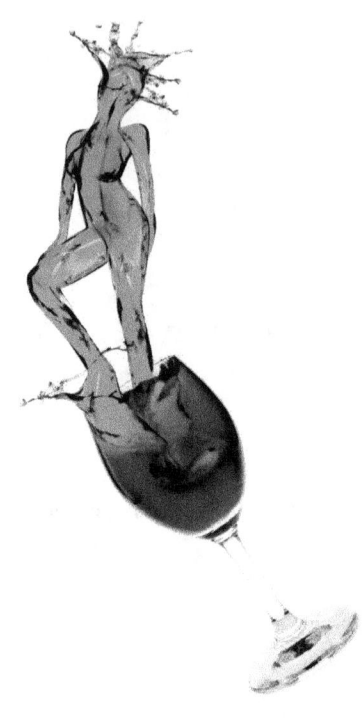

Inebriate Liberally!

Spare not the efforts, my friend!
Pour!
Pour forthwith!
Let your bottomless flask
meet my drunken goblet.

Cohabit

In comfort they reside in us,
our inherent conflicts.

Chip Away

A losing battle it seems;
the wave, ever and anon,
breaking apart on the rocks.

In a thousand years,
find the victor spreading itself
on the languorous beach,
over and over.

Perspective

A mountain tall a thousand miles,
or stands a mite a-front a pebble?
Such are gods, and such are men,
and we know not of whom we speak...

A Footnote in an Ignored Book

The shame of the land
of ten thousand lakes:
a man died of crying thirst.

A Piece Here, A Piece There

The mirrors carry their own world,
and our identity.

Dignity

The mortal spirit strives
for a decent death in life.

The spurned lover's mirror spake

Fickleness, thy name is woman,
Vanity a minor flaw;
frivolous form thy talons have,
coquettish the cutting claws.

Garnish

Must you recall every detail?
Will not some lies satisfy?

Companions

With what facility should I shed these tears?
These tears...
which were my only solace
when you had left...

Pun2

A Mercator map lies with its straight face.

Contra-position

The wine lost the battle
and drowned in his grief.

One Wishes...

To be blessed it must feel,
bequeathed by the lettered fortune
of an ancestral will...

Blind Justice?

Tie as you may, the black blinkers on her eyes!
How would you propose we hide
from that third eye of Truth?

Geometric Credo

Draw a principled circumference.
It locates your steady center.

Seeds

Rotten roots,
bitter fruits.

Tenured

In life you're born a Sisyphus,
destined to keep pushing up the rock,
in hopes, that someday,
you become the rock,
to be pushed up by another Sisyphus...

Janu

Oh, the blinding Simplicity
of Duplicity…

Guidance

One cannot leave the plough
to the bull's own devices.

Write !

Of pencil and chalk...
the treasures of a scribe...

A Thought pre-Launch

A speeding arrow
knows no peace.

Drowned . . .

The orbs,
full of fair spirit,
sit there,
watching in amusement
my spirited resistance...

...and slur with drunken charm:

"He whose lips
hesitate at the cup
never shall he truly taste
the promise of its delicious fate."